Seven Strong

Seven Strong

A South Carolina Poetry
Book Prize Reader

2006–2012

Edited by Kwame Dawes

Foreword by Marjory Wentworth

The University of South Carolina Press

Material from *Keep and Give Away* © 2006 University of South Carolina
Material from *Driving through the Country before You Are Born* © 2007
    University of South Carolina
Material from *Signals* © 2008 University of South Carolina
Material from *How God Ends Us* © 2009 University of South Carolina
Material from *Green Revolver* © 2010 University of South Carolina
Material from *Excavation* © 2011 University of South Carolina
Material from *Hold Like Owls* © 2012 University of South Carolina
New material © 2012 University of South Carolina

Published by the University of South Carolina Press
Columbia, South Carolina 29208

www.sc.edu/uscpress

Manufactured in the United States of America

21 20 19 18 17 16 15 14 13 12   10 9 8 7 6 5 4 3 2 1

Library of Congress Cataloging-in-Publication Data
Seven strong : a South Carolina poetry book prize reader, 2006–2012 /
    edited by Kwame Dawes ; foreword by Marjory Wentworth.
    p. cm.
    ISBN 978-1-61117-093-1 (pbk. : alk. paper)
    1. American poetry—South Carolina. 2. South Carolina—Poetry. I.
Dawes, Kwame Senu Neville, 1962- II. Wentworth, Marjory, 1958-
    PS558.S6S48 2013
    811'.60809757—dc23
                                2012033139

CONTENTS

FOREWORD

South Carolina native Nikky Finney won the 2011 National Book
Award in poetry, and the 2010 winner was Terrance Hayes, also
from South Carolina. This speaks volumes about the deep well
of literary talent that exists in the Palmetto State. Although a va-
riety of styles and subject matter characterize the poems featured
in *Seven Strong*, each poet's voice is equally strong and distinct.
Long known for unique literary voices, South Carolina is home
to the oldest convened state poetry society in the country. This
tradition carries on today, with such nationally known poets as
Susan Ludvigson, Carol Ann Davis, John Lane, Richard Garcia,
and Kurtis Lamkin, among others residing in the state.

In her poem "12th Anniversary on the Appalachian Trail,"
Greenville poet Terri McCord has written: "We are what we re-
member." This line could easily be the epigraph for *Seven Strong*.
Many of the poems in the collection speak to the mysterious
role of memory in the formation of our identities. The role of
culture, geography, and history are intertwined in the South;
and it is impossible to unwind the threads that bind us to this
place. Like it or not, we are tethered to our past. In South Caro-
lina we are quite literally obsessed with it. In many ways we are
still coming to grips with this past. In this way the poems in this
fine collection articulate our collective identity as we experience
a great period of transition.

Ed Madden, for example, is intensely interested in the legacy
of slavery and the Civil War. His poem "Confederates" refers
to a number of incidents tied to race relations in the state—
including the Martin Luther King Day march on Columbia, South
Carolina, in 2000, when almost fifty thousand people marched
to protest the flying of the Confederate flag from the dome of
the State House. His work also recalls an incident in 1970, when

an angry mob of white protesters overturned a bus filled with black school children. At the end of the first stanza, he has quoted a man has been waving a Confederate flag while saying: *Learn your history, / You better learn real history.* We all interpret our history differently, depending on our backgrounds. The irony of this statement is obvious, and it reminds us of the divisions that still exist here. Whether Madden is driving on I-95 or visiting Fort Moultrie on Sullivan's Island, where Africans were held in pest houses before they were sold into slavery in Charleston, over and over again memory and history are tied to place.

Jennifer Pournelle brings that sense of history to her poems about the places in which she has lived and worked throughout the world. Using repeated images, she defines a place by its geology, landscape, and archaeology. The short poem "Jerusalem" is a brilliant meditation on the violence that characterizes that city. In her long tribute to San Diego, "Coscoy, Renamed San Diego," she reminds us how the great sweep of history culminates in the working of the world's great cities, the places where "we live, / and eat and sing and drink and laugh, / and love, and war and cry."

DéLana Dameron is equally fascinated by history. In her introduction, she has written, "I engage poetry and writing as an artistic archival tool," and her poems embody this approach over and over again. Whether she is writing about personal loss or imagining the life of a newly freed slave heading north, there is a defiant sense of joy arising from the suffering and decay that she has described so beautifully. Pulitzer Prize–winning poet and U.S. poet Laureate Natasha Tretheway has spoken of the need for form as a kind of scaffolding when writing about particularly difficult subjects, and Dameron's use of form is spot on. Many of her poems confront the painful realities of witnessing the aging of one's parents. These heartbreaking poems, filled with personal details and actual quotes that come from intense observation, speak to everyone facing this acutely difficult experience.

Susan Laughter Meyers has applied her lyrical gifts to the same subject, achieving a kind of grace that characterizes all her work. Her poem "That Year," which describes the year of her mother's death, uses metaphors found in a garden. Beginning with gorgeous clusters of "black-eyed susans," "moonbeam coreopsis," "lantana," and "narcissus;" and scattering alliteration like petals throughout the poem, she allows readers into her world of grief with a gentle urgency that lingers long after you read the poem. Meyers's technique of naming things in the natural world elevates the language and imbues her poetry with a kind of music. Although she has written about the most ordinary things—dead stumps, dirt, hair and bullfrogs—she continually looks at nature to explain the deepest mysteries of love and death. Born and raised in the South, for her the landscape is profoundly important in these poems, and the role of nature is a hallmark of southern poetic tradition.

As these poets come to grips with their personal histories, they speak to us in ways that resonate beyond the page. The importance of family, again, a particularly southern focus, occurs over and over again on the pages of *Seven Strong*. Poet Ray McManus's coming-of-age poems are honest and tough, but he has managed to look at his childhood and adolescence with a sense of humor. His past is haunted by stories from Ireland, his father's homeland, and a life fraught with violence and unhappiness. These poems, appearing alongside McManus's poems about his own childhood, weave their individual histories inevitably together in ways that are quintessentially southern. The wounds are there, yet these beautifully wrought poems achieve a kind of affirmation despite this. The southern literary tradition of rising from the ruins is readily apparent.

Worthy Evans, a young poet whose work is like no other, often writes about family. The title poem, "Green Revolver," is a fascinating poem about the speaker's son and a plastic green gun his father bought for him. Evans, who served in the U.S. military, deftly reminds us of the power of a revolver and its ultimate purpose. Everything is heightened in Evans's poems, which always celebrate the ordinary— from cartoons and *Mad Magazine* to teamwork classes at work. Even body odor deserves a poem in Worthy Evans's world. But the last Evans's poem in *Seven Strong*, "The Madman's Divining Time," will remind readers of Susan Meyer's poem "That Year." The subject may not be the same, but the garden setting and actions of Mona, working "her thumbs into the pots / of petunias, pansies, marigolds," echo those of Meyers's speaker, whose hands are "working the dirt, a dark loam / that would spring into jonquils, daffodils—bright / coronas of yellow."

Memories of growing up in South Carolina inspire poet Julia Koets, whose work is filled with images from her childhood. Her poem "Joy, the Elephant, Greenville Zoo, 1990," recalls visits to the zoo with her grandmother and brother. Without using the words *summer, heat,* or *drought,* Koets's brilliant imagery places us at the zoo during the dog days of a southern summer, passing the elephant's cage "at the top of the hill: pool / dirty with up-country clay, two tires scattered / in dust, a few blocks of hay to keep the ground / from running when it rained." Her ability to capture particular sensory details yields a palpable sense of immediacy, creating poems as individual and enduring as photographs.

I cannot imagine the world without these books, and I am eternally grateful to Kwame Dawes and Charlene Spearen for all of the work they did at the South Carolina Poetry Initiative. They were tireless in their efforts on behalf of poets in the state. The seven books resulting from the South Carolina Poetry Book Prize are a testament to the work of the SC Poetry Initiative.

Marjory Wentworth
South Carolina Poet Laureate

INTRODUCTION

There is a peculiar truth about the power of publishing: if books are not published, there is an odd sense that nothing worth repeating or preserving has been said. One can imagine a time when this privileging of the published word did not define value in society, but alas, we live, for the most part, in a different world.

Poetry has flourished in South Carolina for a very long time, but the publishing of South Carolina poets has largely been left to out-of-state publishers. There is a certain pride that one can take in this—our writers, after all, are good enough to be published outside the state. The problem, of course, is that the myth of the pure poem published for its universally accepted strengths is a heady one, but one that we must always challenge and debunk if we are to ensure that the work of gifted poets is published. Publishers publish what they imagine will sell, and what they happen to like. We like things for very arbitrary reasons, and these have less to do with universally accepted poetic standards than we care to admit. Regional biases, stylistic biases, racial biases, ideological biases, gender biases, and sexual biases all figure into what is published in our country today. And this is why, one can fairly argue, the publishing of poetry is a dynamic and lively enterprise in the United States today. Democracy, it may argued, is achieved when a world of biased people find a way to live together peacefully. It is such a bias that led to the South Carolina Poetry Book Prize.

Knowing that much wonderful poetry was being written by poets who call this state home, Charlene Spearen and I, as the coconspirators in the work of the South Carolina Poetry Initiative, decided to find a way to celebrate this work by offering a contest judged by gifted poets with national and international standing, and then publishing the winners with a reputable press willing to take a chance on a poetry series.

The making of this argument was simplified by the awareness that the University of South Carolina Press was explicitly candid about its reluctance to take on a new poetry project. The last one had not done as well as they had hoped, and, and by the time the series was discontinued, the press was understandably gun-shy about publishing poetry.

So we made an offer to the press that we felt would be hard for them to refuse. We offered to administer the contest at all levels and assume all costs related to the planning of the contest. We guaranteed the sell-out of the first print run of the winning book. We offered to serve as publicists for the poets and their books. We promised to make much of the fact that this book was a prize-winning book, an immediate pretext for publicity and media attention. We guaranteed the endorsement of at least one nationally renowned poet—namely the judge. We offered to handle the editorial work on the book. Finally, we offered to find subvention funds for the production of the book. Our offer combined with the design, publicity, cataloguing, copyediting, and credibility branding that the press would provide, not to mention the all-too-expensive distribution cost and management made this a formidable partnership. The press agreed, and the South Carolina Poetry Book Prize was launched.

The English Department at the University of South Carolina was supportive of this project, and each year committed funds to support the subvention costs for the publication. The rest was easy. The poets submitted their manuscripts, the judges judged, and quality books were made each year, adding to the body of work that one could call South Carolinian.

Ours is not a first-book prize, but tellingly, for most of our winners, this publication has constituted their debut full-length poetry collection. Our judges have been a special boost for the prize. Any book series that has been introduced and selected by Terrance Hayes, Afaa Weaver, David Baker, Nikky Finney,

Elizabeth Alexander, Riggoberto Gonzalez, and Kate Daniels is not one to sniff at. Yet each of these judges has been a generous and conscientious partner in the project, writing elegant commentaries on each of the winning collections and lending their names to the fate of the collections. Beyond that, the success of the series has been driven by the enterprising and accommodating spirit of the poets themselves, who have worked hard to sell their books and to lend the series a high profile.

The work written by these seven poets both proves and shatters the notion of a southern aesthetic. These are strikingly distinctive voices, but the fact that they come from this state reminds us that ideas of what is southern and what is South Carolinian have to be constantly reassessed, and these collections are wonderfully different in their interests and focus.

Susan Laughter Meyers's graceful courage in treating with unblinking honesty and revelation the complexities of losing a parent and discovering the divide between ourselves and those who produced us in her collection is work treats the landscape of the lowcountry of South Carolina, not as a bit of local color but as an elemental source of metaphor and image for her poems.

Ray MacManus on the other hand has written with the spare blunt efficiency of a poet with a wry sense of the world. But his vision is not cynical. Indeed he has detailed his rural southern upbringing with a contemporary clarity— a world of violence, meth labs, encroaching suburbia, and dysfunction. Yet what stands out in these poems is the poet's complete belief in the salvific power of poetry, the capacity of the poem to transform the individual no matter where he comes from.

Ed Madden's verse arrives thick with a sensual attentiveness to the physical world, and, for Madden, the details of flowers, the farm, and the way gardens are tended offer an intimate path into a world in which race, sexual identity, religion, and the complications of family provide the fodder for a poetic mastery that manages to make the use of form seem effortless and necessary, almost inevitable.

DéLana Dameron's meditations on faith, identity, and the politics of relationships are handled with an expansive wit and a poetic ambition that grows out of her intense commitment to what she sees as an important connection between the role and function of a historian as an archivist and that of a poet, studying the world and somehow, through the preserving agent of poetic form, finding ways to present ideas to others. Her sense of the South is assured in its sophistication—cliches, stereotypes, and tired tropes are simply not welcome here.

For Worthy Evans, however, both the internal and external sense of place is very confined and specific—it is the world of a twenty-first century office where a man tries to hold down a job in an environment that is eroding his sense of security and his understanding of masculinity and identity. But there is no alarm in these poems, simply an understanding that in the hands of a quirky, gifted poet with an uncanny capacity to observe and then to filter out those things that are most intriguing and engaging, something as mundane as a nondescript office can be a cultural gold mine for poetic expression. Evan's deadpan humor is unsettling largely because it never announces itself, leaving us wondering if our labeling what he is doing as humor is not merely our way of calming what we fear in ourselves.

And where Evans has constricted his sense of the physical world, Jennifer Pournelle's impressive experience as an engaged and thoughtful traveler informs the worlds that she has created. Her verse is meticulous, precise, and sharply honed as she creates studies that are rooted in her fulsome understanding of history, and her own engagement in the geopolitics of a world in which wars are being fought in places with long and complex histories of destruction. At no point, however, do we lose our sense of being transported by a poet who has found emotional power in the archaeological details of worlds that may seem alien to us until we read the poems.

Julia Koets poems remain rooted in the United States, but their clean, slim efficiency, their tenderly observed understanding of human relationships, and their effortless and most natural syntax offer us a poetics that feels entirely contemporary and yet wholly rooted in the poetic legacies of Edith Sitwell and Emily Dickinson. Julia Koets's poems are small, delicate gems that offer so much with each reading.

It is therefore impossible to try to suggest that these poets are committed to some kind of guiding regional aesthetic. Part of the reason for this eclectic mix of voices is the fact that we have managed to involve judges with quite distinctive tastes and interests. And, as a result, the poetry that has been published is able to reflect that in beautiful ways.

This selection was one that took a great deal of effort on my part largely because there were so many poems that I wanted to include and that I simply could not because of the limitations of space. But, having made the selections, and having allowed a week or so to go by, I returned to the manuscript to read it through, and what I found was a delightful journey into what I felt were the keynotes, themes, and stylistic approaches of each of these poets. In a sense this is a sampler, a rich, satisfying sampler that has the peculiar benefit of consisting of poems that are self-contained and that manage to create their own universe of thought and feeling.

Seven Strong constitutes the kind of artistic reward that comes from collaboration and imagination. Jonathan Haupt, newly appointed director of the University of South Carolina Press, came up with this brilliant idea of somehow showcasing the work of our book-prize winners in a single anthology. In so doing, he has sent a message that the University of South Carolina Press understands the value of poetry in a society, and especially in the state of South Carolina. More than that, however, he has shown an appreciation of just how gifted these poets are and how beautiful these books of poems are. He is affirming what I have always believed and what I continue to believe about the poets of South Carolina.

Kwame Dawes

Lincoln, Nebraska

PART 1

Keep and Give Away (2006)

Susan Laughter Meyers

"*Keep and Give Away* offers us countless resounding, delicate notes. We might fall, submit to loss, were there no art such as this to keep us upright in the world."

Terrance Hayes, author of *Wind in a Box* and *Hip Logic*, from his foreword

Standing Ajar

For me, to write a poem means to shake off the rational and step outside of time, when something within me opens up. Emily Dickinson said it best: "The soul should always stand ajar, ready to welcome the ecstatic experience." So I try to follow Emily's advice and keep myself available to whatever might arrive.

I'm most apt to start with a line, maybe one that pops into my head or words overheard in a passing conversation—there's no telling where that line might come from. And, of course, there's no telling where the poem might go. My hope is that I have the good sense to allow it to go where it pleases, that I don't try to coax it down some predetermined path. More often than not the observable world will make its way into the poem, because paying attention is my job as a poet.

Nothing pleases me more than naming what's before me. *Wren, pickerelweed, laughing gull, sumac. Blouse, rail, bushel basket, kitchen window.* Memory usually shows up, too—as it does in many of the poems in *Keep and Give Away*—sometimes coupled with imagination and happenstance. (These things aren't planned.)

Depending on the poem, a walk may be in order, or I may turn to a favorite resource—one of several dictionaries, a thesaurus, a field guide or two, an old journal entry, Google—though that seems to happen more frequently now than it did with my poems in this anthology.

Regardless of the practical and physical circumstances, ultimately for me the process is about wanting to be astonished. If I'm lucky, there's some sort of shift to the interior, some sort of surprise, no matter how slight or slow to arrive. If I'm lucky—and persistent.

Susan Laughter Meyers

Your Mother Forbids You
to Leave the Yard

You sit in your swing, like a loose limb
dangling from the biggest branch
which knows trunk, which knows ground.

You pump and stretch, kicking up
speed on this furious horse
until you soar past your neighbor's garage.

Below you the dog wags his tail. Inside,
the old clock travels the day,
its pendulum sweeping hill valley hill.

Whoosh is the song in your ear, wind
then mutinous hair in your face.
Comes the wind again, forgiving

as a mother watching at the window,
her arms folded, wishing
away love's daily punishments.

The morning moon wears lace, white
as your grandmother's hair.
You laugh and touch it with your toe.

Lean back into the rhapsody of air.
Lost child, close your eyes.
Let the wide sky lap you up, and up.

That Year

for my mother

When the black-eyed susans begin to bloom
in the backyard, and the moonbeam coreopsis
bursts into tiny stars, I think of the year

I banished yellow from my life. It was the year
I dug up the lantana, when I didn't plant
narcissus and all the buttery bulbs

but chose white, and a little blue, for the garden
without knowing that I was readying
for two long years of her dying. The next spring

I painted our kitchen, once a lemony gloss, ecru.
I threw out from my closet all the blouses
hinting, from their hangers, of glad canaries.

Beginning that fall I dressed in a dull haze
of beige, toning myself down for the end.
I ignored the incandescence of morning, the amber

of dusk, and leaned to clouds billowed in black.
The week in November she died I loaded the trunk
of my car with flats of pansies, three sacks of bulbs.

I wanted my hands working the dirt, a dark loam
that would spring into jonquils, daffodils—bright
coronas of yellow, and yellow, and yellow.

Washing the Breakfast Dishes, I Decide

. . . what noun
would you want
spoken on your skin
your whole life through?
            Mark Doty

Wren. I considered
open-mouthed words—*love,*
honor, even *melancholy*
for the sound of it—
afraid I might waste
this chance, like the one wish.
Then I remembered last Thursday's
small brown bird on the rail,
its head tilted back
in what I imagined sudden joy,
though I know its trill,
sweet and full,
rose from the breast of instinct,
the throat of an ordinary day.

Daughter

I will fly you to the city.
Stars will light the black
sky as you land.

       That's a lie.

    Expect more light
    than dark can hold.

You must learn to live with it
like dreams stacked in the corner.
Sleep with your eyes open.

I will send you to the mountains
where a breeze sketches your face,
daisies bleach the lower slopes,
moss tempers the north side.

Lie down and close your eyes.

If I say *yellow*, do you feel
on your lids the silk of the sun?
        I say *red*.

Never depend on light
to render the shapes you need.

Awaiting My Brother's Pathology Report, My Husband and I Take to the River

for Gene

Laughing gulls laugh, and laugh, what they do best.
Hilarious, I guess, the afternoon sun.
They can barely contain themselves. A pageant
of cedar, Chinese tallow, more cedar.
                              I'm half sick
of all this beauty. Grapevines thread
the bank's bramble. An osprey repeats its pitiful call—
odd, its small cry.

             Blue stands at the bow
and whips his line past a bumblebee droning
from rod to unused rod propped up against the seat.
Fish crows talk their low crow talk.
                    The bee buzzes
so near my head (almost touching my nape) I cringe
and break out in goose bumps.

                    Here's the hope:
a dried-up vine clings to whatever it can.
Still there, a wrecked boat and motor,
half submerged, left to rust. A stand of sumac,
that determined weed.

Dead stumps dot the water.
We have come here to ease through something green
and growing.

Is that a bullfrog, or alligator,
bellowing low? Out here the birds are kind
with their remarks, pickerelweed thrives

in clumps.
Full to crested over, what does the river care?
A frog jumps from the bank in its long, perfect arc.
Blue switches bait. Above us a grackle
fusses and flits from limb to limb.

Keep and Give Away

What do I know of man's destiny?
I could tell you more about radishes.
                              Samuel Beckett

With a bushel basket in hand
he's the tally of my ripest desires,

more than the sum of his summer
crops, perfect and plentiful as they are

even counting Early Contenders
and Silver Queen. Burpless

cucumbers, Kentucky Wonders, too.
Throw in the fruit to sweeten

the numbers: blackberries and figs
piled in pyramids or weighed

in pecks. And don't forget
the peppers (red, yellow, green),

divided into *keep* and *give away.*
Dinner plates—heaped with leafiness,

tubers, and pods——heavy
with the haul and roots of his labor.

Now he's shelling peas in his lap
and I sit across the room, listening

to the ping, ping. He's more
than the sum, I cannot count the ways,

and despite a constant reckoning
of work and luck, numbers fail me

in this long, hot growing season.

PART 2

Driving through the Country before You Are Born (2007)

Ray McManus

"What we take away from this book is the poet's solace in the quiet solitude of the writer at work, searching for the temporary consolations of the right word in the right place, and the power of that small act——made over and over again——to keep us alive and to keep us writing."

Kate Daniels, author of *The White Wave, The Niobe Poems,* and *Four Testimonies,* from her foreword

One Good Apple

When I was teenager, I used to run a chainsaw for ten dollars an hour. I started when I was fourteen, and I worked with some tough guys. Bad asses and dumb asses really—always telling me stories about blisters and the weakness of human skin. I never knew if they were kidding with me, so I believed everything they said, and I learned to hold my own. I had to. There wasn't much room for error. At wide-open throttle, the teeth of a chainsaw become an unforgiving blur. There were times when the whir of the wood chipper and the whine of the saw would harmonize, and I found a certain beauty in that. It got to where I wanted to hear it more than I was willing to pay attention. I have the scars to show for it.

In college I stacked apples in a grocery store. Red Delicious, Golden Delicious, and Granny Smith apples, misshapen bricks of flesh that bruise too easy when dropped or rolled on the cement floor of the produce department, stay best when cross-stacked, stems pointed in one direction every other row. I could stack them high and wide, and the customers would tear into them, leaving little for me to rebuild with.

But they were common apples. I always liked the Braeburns, the Fujis, and the Honey Crisps, apples most people never heard of. They were tougher to stack, and harder to sell. It didn't matter what sign I created, it didn't matter how many baskets I added to the display, most of the customers looked at me as if I were trying to sell them poison.

So I would go to the back and cut apples into slices and walk around the store handing them out. Customers would look surprised, smile, and buy apples four at a time. Some would say something about how good the display looked. Others just commented on how this apple was the best apple they had ever eaten. They always thanked me. But no one ever thought to ask me if I bothered to wash my hands.

Ray McManus

Black

When I was fourteen and my pop quoted Yeats
for the last time in his loaded Irish accent,
my grandmother stood there trembling in blackness
wringing out the tears that ran across
the creases of her yellow over-ripened face.
I was just a boy in my own blackness,
my lungs blackened from each Drum I rolled,
thinking of my pop and his bitter, black coffee.
When I was seven, he taught me about custody
and culture, a hand-me-down story of how
he burned, or rather ran with those who burned,
a Protestant shop in Enniskillen, a story
about ashes, about never going back
to see Ulster's black sky, his mother, his father,
his eldest boy in the blackness, in the graves.

Burning Caterpillars

In spring Pop would say, "time to burn the bastards,"
and I would watch his withered body climb ladders,
raise torches, burn fuzzy sacks from the pecan trees.
At that age, it was all about the burning,
the consumption, the fire, and somehow I
managed to take my place without thinking
about trees or fire, without thinking
about anything, saying the word *bastard*
over and over again until I
could see it take shape, climb up the ladder.

But the thought is ash now, remnants of a fire that burned
out a long time ago—an old man, a tree stump,
hollowed and rotten, weaker than the other trees.

Back then, I played in the dirt, never thought
about a dad planting trees, how they burn,
keep us warm on cold nights. I was a bastard
by any definition: I wouldn't climb the ladder,
didn't give a damn who I was or where I
came from then, now, all the changes in between. I
remember times Pop took me to the big trees,
their limbs sagging in the middle, the ladder

rocking while globs of burning jelly fell on my head,
and for the first time I felt like a bastard,
kept my head down, ignored the burning.
Sometimes I take my finger, rub it where fire has burned
and left its mark, its ash scattered over dirt I
have long since forgotten. I'm the only bastard
here. There were days after first frost, when trees
were barren, almost dead, and Pop thought
they were too small, that he didn't need a ladder,
or someone to help him climb. I was the ladder

holding a feeble man high on a burning
pedestal so a boy might grow up not thinking
about what he puts in his mouth. When I
stand, I fall down. When I carve words on tree
stumps, they talk back at me. Words like *bastard,
barren, burning*——reminders that I killed something,
a thought perhaps, something about trees,
a bastard, an old ladder left leaning too long.

Orientation

You see that man. He is your boss.
He will tell you to bend over
and pick up the loose Temple
orange that rolls on the floor.
And you will. And you will
hand it to him, and he will
wipe the blade of his knife
using the bottom of his apron,
and cut the orange into four equal
pieces. And he will not give you one.

Red Barn

I

In the morning, before the sun
collars the trunks of large oaks,
something else rises without permission.
I squirm from it like it's
some kind of irritation—sand
in the bed, a crooked mirror on the wall—
and call it the awakening. But it's just another
affirmation of what I don't have
beside me, what I won't find in the closet,
what I can't see beyond the dust
flittering in the sunlight around
the Mason jar on the ruddy brown dresser.

II

If I am awake, I hope that it was
just a dream, something I can cling to
when the water hits my back.
I am heavy. Under the covers
there is a way out, a possibility, a rub.
She is beautiful and soft.
I stroke and beat and press down
with my thumb to hold back the eruption,
think about beach sand in the joints, the salt
in the corners of my mouth. I take
my tongue lick the edges, see
the weeds in her hair, smell
the ocean in her skin, feel
the soft folds, the hard lines with each thrust,
the moist center . . . release.

It is time.

III

There is nothing I can say
about the way things smell
on Sunday mornings: chicken
smells like chicken, fried gravy
smells like fried gravy. Perhaps
I could point out what smells
like ash and what smells like dirt,
but the lid kept tight on the pot
becomes what I hear:
a comfortable hiss, a crackle,
a pop, the absence of water
on hot steel, the small silences.

IV

The sun shows the gaps in the planks,
makes walls look like they are closing in.
I want to run outside but I find myself
looking somewhere past the wheelbarrow,
ladder, hoes and shovels; beyond the barrels,
ropes, rakes, and chains; behind old doors,
plaster casts, sheets of glass and slate.
I find the feathers and the dark spots
in the dirt, old stories about baby chicks
pecked to death by older chickens
because of the simple specks of difference.
And then it starts. The inevitable whimper
that turns to drone, turns to rhythm,
turns to sounds I have heard
before, sounds that I never want
to hear again: dirt slung in the bottom
of a jar, a fist rubbed against the reeds,
the belt on Trudy's back. And I
know my time is going to come.
The wolves are at the door.

V

I rub the blade against the ridges on my thumb
slow enough so that the edge catches each one.
I stop at the center, hold there, apply pressure.

Point of view is clear in the field, there is nothing
between me and the horizon, but a house, a kitchen
window. I watch the mother die. I watch the son blame
himself. I watch the father look down. There is no other
way to remember it. I can reach into my pockets,
dig for old roaches; think it is time to start tearing
the old man down, but he will still wrap the strap
tighter around his forearm, and I will flinch
the same way Trudy flinches, finger the small
welts, the thin barriers between interior
and exterior, and watch the way skin responds
to pain with fluid, the way blood strains just under
the surface to let me know it is there.

His eyes are closed. I keep the house always
to my back, the mouth of the row tight and even,
and let the blade slowly close the throat.

VI

In the back, there is a lump.
The collapse is inevitable.
A pile will break down, decompose
like a kid's dream hid in the leaves——
give it time.
When wheat dies, it falls forward.
I am the earth. I cannot tell
the difference between hard and soft,
only constants. I dig the hole, listen
to metal slice the dirt. It is not enough.
The ground is stubborn, returns its shape,
won't bend under pressure, won't give
to weight, and the horizon is slowly moving
in. Still I dig, try not to talk about concussions,
unnecessary bruising, slicing the knuckle off
to gain a few extra inches, or the miles of rows
left unfinished.

VII

I fill the hole cover.
Move forward.

The rats are in the corn.
The old man is dead.

What is buried is buried.
I can go back to sleep.

Driving through the Country
before You Are Born

Objects may be closer than they appear.
Don't think about what they are saying behind your back.
Go to school. Eat regularly.
Say what you mean. Don't spit.
If it's offered, take it. Don't split
your want-to's and your have-to's.
Don't eat the red berries that grow
behind your grandmother's house;
they will make you sick
more than you should ever know.
Don't think about what the air should smell like.
Don't think about what house should go where.
Don't think about what you have until you are at least 25.

Live your own life until you're 25. When you're 25,
you'll look back, wonder where it went
and where it was supposed to go. When you're 25,
you won't think you are really 25, part your hair
25 different ways, find 25 different reasons
for not paying bills, think about 25 different answers
for every question that makes you feel
uncomfortable, wake up 25 times
a night, realize that you've turned 37.

Remember that your father once helped
an old lady fix a flat tire on the side of the road.
Remember that he saw her two years later
in a grocery store. She did not recognize him.
Remember that it took him three more years
to figure out that it didn't matter.

Don't talk with your mouth full
of nothing surprising. Don't wait
to be asked if you have something
to say. Don't tell anyone
about your aches, your boredom, your efforts,
your pain. Stay away from grocery stores
with bad lighting. If it's not broke,
fix it. Don't jump on the bed
unless you really mean it. If you must climb
ladders, don't spit on those below you,
and if you do, do not stand on anything flimsy.

You will make enemies.
You will love them.
You will find them attractive,
though you will not like what you see.
You'll know what it's like to hate.
You'll know when they are saying something
behind your back, and you'll learn
the right way to do the wrong thing.
You'll think it's not worth it, and drive away.

PART 3

Signals (2008)

Ed Madden

"*Signals* combines a matter-of-fact lyrical eye with a view to harder social realities, and there is a consistency in the collection, a working with and around couplets and tercets, a sparseness that seems to match an arid landscape, a place where one searches for hope. This collection bears the evidence of a high level of craft alongside a concern for what goes on in our lives."

Afaa Weaver, author of *The Plum Flower Dance: Poems, 1985–2005,* from her foreword

Frog Eyes

In tenth-grade biology, I learned that the world I took for granted was not to be taken for granted, that the phenomenologies of sense——the bright gold of goldenrod in October, the gritty taste of blackberries from the roadside, the viscid loll of a tadpole in my palm, the thick and fishy smell of the ditch near the house going dry——were not enough. There were names for things and things to know. A small mammal skull from a field could become a project on taxonomy and teeth. The aquarium at the back of the lab wasn't for goldfish and guppies: it became my display of native things: freshwater shrimp, bullfrog tadpoles, a tiny gar rescued from the ditch, all teeth and tail. A puddle of wriggling things in a ditch going dry could become an ecological microcosm. A story about my father, about a trot line in the river and trash fish on the line, was only one way to know the world: learning the names for things was another.

There were arrowheads in the field behind my house, something to pick up, drop in your pocket. Everyone had an Indian grinding rock in a flowerbed. Memory and history aren't the same thing.

When I moved to South Carolina in 1994, I quickly learned that the South was not a single thing. I thought Arkansas was the South——now I'm not so sure. There are many versions of the South. In Gilbert, the woman who sold us flowers from her backyard added a clump of blue flowers for free——a blue spiderwort we'd admired. It looked like the dayflower from my mom's backyard. My mom lets it grow for the pretty blue flowers. My aunt Elaine says mow it down: "That's just snaky, right here at the back door. The woman in Gilbert put a clump of them in a plastic grocery bag." "Frog eyes," she added.

There were names for things, things to know.

Ed Madden

Trough ✕

Cowlake, Arkansas, 1969

For the horses, in the run between the barn and the pasture,
where a catalpa tree bears its crop of worms. What draws you?

Constant tug of the dark water, the still water, its insides
tin and slick with green. Almost as tall as you are and——

your cousin warns——big enough to drown in. Just inside
the barbed wire that snags you when you lean over to stir

the darkness, to stare at the fish, enormous fish in the
    dark water,
gold and black, rising like apparitions to the surface,

where you scatter oatmeal stolen from your grandma's
    cupboards,
an offering, a secret. The fish come to you, bidden, hungry.

They are everywhere. They are always hungry.

What I Found

Keowee-Toxaway State Park, March 2006

I

How long can you stare at the lake?
How long can you stare at the sky?

A boat's wake massages the shore.

In the sand, driftwood, limbs
and roots worn smooth, numb.

Take the largest piece you can
carry back to the cabin.

Place it on the porch like a totem.

II

A small black conical shell, splinter the water left.

Alder cones, resurrection plant, the dried pipsissewa.
A merkin of moss.

A scorpion, tail raised in threat, dry and dead,
near the cabin door.

A branch of forsythia in bloom, placed
in a dark olive wine bottle.

A little red rubber fish: child's toy, evidence.

III

The windows are dark. The light makes a circle
of mossy lawn just beyond the door.

On the radio someone sings, *Who says you can't go home?*
I haven't spoken to my father in a decade.

The lake is a darkness behind the night's darkness.
The rain isn't here yet, but will be soon.

Inventory

The Audubon prints, the English china,
the flamingo painting, the lacquer trays——

several lists of Sam's possessions
lie on the table of his former lover—

a sewing machine, the Soloflex,
imported sweaters, a box of books,

the chifforobe, large and ornate,
heavy wood of a polished coffin.

Each page has a name at the top of a list.
The elder brother, who hopes to close

the affair soon, is recipient of Sam's
collection of monkeys, decorated boxes,

an ebony bowl. The sister rejects
the bedroom suite, the princess dresser,

the wardrobe and all that he has left her
(though not the clothes she's already taken).

She wants the green sofa, will have
nothing else. So strange the way

grief is manifested as greed.
No one claimed the porn: it disappeared

the day of the funeral. Sam hoped
to curse his lover with joy, left him

the boxes of holiday ornaments, though
the sister must have those things, too,

stores them now with the Empire chairs,
the gazing globe, blue as a bruise.

To others he leaves the Polynesian figures,
the end table shaped like an Indian slave,

who holds a platter of glass on his head—
he kneels to offer a collection of snapshots,

ex-lover and friends in Halloween drag
(pirate, vampire, courtesan, queen),

and a framed photo of San Francisco,
a bridge spanning waves of fog,

and paradise on the other side, waiting,
the streets of gold, the gates of pearl.

Confederates

going north on I-95, March 2000

Bert stops at the BP for gas.
I go in for coffee while he pays.
He's fixing to say something, but doesn't——
the television above us stops him,
a man with a flag saying: *Learn your history.*
You better learn real history.

After the march, a woman asked us: *Where you from?*
Meaning, why are nice young men like you
marching with *them,* the river of black folk
purling around us, the flag
a bright flame in the cold sky.

Early March and we watch the road unfurl
behind us. We tell each other stories:
only boys when it all happened——
that bus full of kids overturned
by a white mob on a Darlington County road,
or that girl in Arkansas, escorted into school with guns.

To us, that flag's just something to do
with Lynyrd Skynyrd, old pickup trucks,
guys with long hair and tight jeans.

A gray fog haunts the highway.
Bert adjusts the rearview mirror.
Our friends are waiting at the next exit.

Signals

Fort Moultrie, January 2005

Four white ibis hunch on the yardarm——
the naval signal flags long gone——

just four white birds, their beaks tucked,
the winter sun cold and bright,

the fort's one flag snapping in the wind.

On the beach, sandpipers test the surf's edge,
pick through the detritus of tourist and tide.

You point to the dolphin out in the channel,
beyond it Fort Sumter, distant ruin.

Black breakers reach like arms out into the rough water.

In the parking lot, we smell the marsh beyond us,
and the sweetness of a tea olive nearby.

A bare tree suddenly blossoms in blackbird——
strange fruit shining in the morning sun.

A sulfur butterfly blows across the lawn.

PART 4

How God Ends Us (2009)

DéLana R. A. Dameron

"Her speakers are ruthless with the poem-making self but filled with compassion for the world they encounter."

Elizabeth Alexander, presidential inaugural poet and author of *American Sublime*, from her foreword.

Relics and Artifacts

Windsor Elementary School in Columbia had a publishing press in the back corner of the library. I took what I didn't know were called "manuscripts" at the time to the librarian and picked out my cover design. She typed and bound each of my manuscripts and sent a note to my classroom when they were ready for pick up. At five years old, I started my love affair with archiving, with writing my life, with living as a writer.

What is most significant about the books, and perhaps my decision to become a writer, is my concern, even then, to make my words a relic or artifact. They were not fictional stories. They were books about my family, about myself. What was a concession to my father's argument about "objective careers" only reinforced my writing. I majored in third world and non-western history in college and engaged in what I called a type of "translation." The Coptic poet Matthew Shenoda says in his collection of poetry, *Somewhere Else*, to "tell the story of somewhere else." I have taken this line and applied it to my career and charge as a poet, a human, an activist, a translator of history.

Saadi Simawe speaks of literal translation in the introduction to Dunya Mikhail's *The War Works Hard*. He says that a translator working in two different languages should have, "the irresistible urge to possess the text by rewriting it in [her] native tongue." Understanding this, I knew that to view myself as a translator, I must encompass wholly this idea. I must negotiate the two languages of my peers: the historical vernacular that holds the inaccessible narratives from the common reader and the creative/imaginary world of literature, both of which I claim as my own.

I engage poetry and writing as an artistic archival tool. As a historian, I appreciate the importance of art and how it serves as an artifact when monuments are gone and flesh decays. I write with the past, present, and future in mind. I write cognizant that each word is at once a statement, a testament, a music chord, a relic.

DéLana R. A. Dameron

Lament

Oh, how You end us.
The beginning of disaster
is the moist inside of a lie. How You
speak with fiery tongue, with smoke words. How You
hide spirits in the spaces of the house no one inhabits.
There are other silences You keep.

There are other silences You keep
about the way You will end us
or send spirits in the spaces of the house no one inhabits.
The beginning of disaster: Your
fiery tongue-speak. Words fly up in smoke,
curl inside-out to reveal the moist parts of a lie.

Inside the tender part——the stomach of a lie——
are other kept silences. How You twirl
Your fiery tongue. Your words are smoke.
But, how You'll end us,
summon spirits from inhabitable spaces
to whisper the beginnings of disaster.

Curled in the beginning of disaster,
deep inside the moist, tender parts are words
fired from Your tongue. All smoke.

Cull the spirits from the dark spaces of the house.
Cull them from the silences we keep.
God. The end of us.

You'll soon end us.
It will be the beginning of a disaster.
Speak now with Your tongue of fire and smoke words.
Unearth the underbelly of all lies.
Inside the silences You keep
are spirits in the spaces of the house

where no one dwells, in the crevices
where You'll surely end us—
here, in the silences of the house, the silences kept.
It will be the beginning and the end. Disaster
is the tender, moist center of every lie.
Still, Your tongue is fire. Our words, mere smoke.

It Is Written

Daddy is approaching fifty. I fret
because it was his father's age
at death. All he desired of life
was to surpass his father.
Fifty-one is the only limit left to hurdle.

Six states away he watches his last living blood
turn rock and disintegrate. He calls,
hesitation constricts his words   *I don't know*
if you know, but   he is aware my knowledge
comes from what he wills over the line,
the distances between us.

He begins to cry   *Maybe you'll write*
a poem about   but I know he means, soon
there will be no one to tell the story.
He dictates   *It's funny, Mom never wanted to die*
in a nursing home.   She spent weeks
in his house and he washed her, fed her.
She always said 'you're a man
once but a child twice.'

He grabs the air. *My baby brother*
is a child twice. He cannot live
in his own house.

I don't mention karma or God's vengeance,
how Grandma couldn't spend her last days
at home because the same brother refused
to care for her. *He is going—*
I fill the blank with: *to die?*
But the space is: *to a nursing home.*
Daddy whimpers   *His skin is falling off his legs,*
he cannot care for his self.
I think about the law of God. An eye for an eye.
He starts again: *Maybe you'll write—*
And I say *Yes, yes.*

Body, an Elegy

Suddenly the body says night.
Cyrus Cassells

The body is not
an insomniac, some
twilight sleepless walker.
It turns to lie down
as it pleases, at times
against your will.

The body chooses
its separate departures
to backrooms of the house.
Goodnight heel, boomerang
of bone and tendons.
Goodnight feet, arch-less
pestle-crush of earth.

The doctors come
to chop you down
and cover you with strips
of white linen. See,
your legs, your trunks
of redwoods stripped
of their flesh bark
are endangered. Goodnight
kidney, fallen already

to a deep coma,
needing machines to eat
and drink. For it,
there is no waking.

Your left arm long
retired and under the
sheets. Uncle, lay
your perfect right
that never knew shunt
or needle, lay it down
so the I. V. can land. Together,
we say goodnight to the heart
that has failed you once.

But the eyes, they refuse.
Your mouth does not
wish to go so soon. So
speak your farewells, Uncle.
Speak your hundred more
farewells. Watch this holy
body of birds flap
across your window.

On Seeking the Other ²/₅ Up North ✝

after Patricia Smith, based on her nineteenth-century portrait

First thing you do when you find free
is pose, take a picture in the stiff double-breasted
overcoats buttoned to the top.

First thing you do when you find free
is wash up, scrape years of top soil
baked onto skin, pray the grime in the bottom
of the basin (years' work in the dirt) can be forgiven.

You find free from southern sun,
take pictures, pose like white men, and even build
a house with mantles; dangle from the walls.

Yes, you slip your right hand
into the jacket up to the second
knuckle, just between the buttons,
snug like love into an envelope.

You pose, don't mention anything
about your roots, no, they have cut
your hair so close your scalp can breathe.

You will not smile.
Your look will be a flash into history:
your proof you made it out those fields.

Inheritance

after Lucille Clifton

Frequented in dreams
by fresh-dead loves, so I have seen
with these eyes the eyes of a spirit
who has crossed, seen the body reject
its coffin bed and climb right out
onto the church's plank floor
seen the dove at the bed's foot
calling out all names, or the red eyes
of the flesh, abandoned. Do not say
I should be grateful for perfect eyes
or their ability to see such distances.
Say I should be grateful for sight,
for open and shut.

The City of Discarded Umbrellas

Why do assemblies of umbrellas
always occur in London?
    Neruda, The Book of Questions

There are assemblies of the shattered
in Harlem, too. Umbrellas, broken
in the trashcans, upended

on the sidewalk, teeter
on the curb, the lip of a city under siege.
There are assemblies of abandoned umbrellas
that have given up their dance,

cannot twirl their skirts
above the heads of their travelers.
Even in the rain, in the relentless
beating of the sky, they congregate

on the corners with broken legs,
with broken backs, their feet calloused, unable to walk.

Flame ✳

When you meet a man who is satisfied
with one match to start a fire

that should last one thousand days,
you want to be the wall wind

cannot pass through, to be as wide
as a brick house around his singular hearth.

When you meet this man, you want
to be the dry kindling and you wait

for the touch, the blue of his fire.
This man's love is a final flame

held over you, and you say that you will
burn. You will. Here is your body that burns

for him. Here is the ash: your used-up self,
what's left to be swept away.

PART 5

t/_

Green Revolver (2010)

Worthy Evans

"This poet is a shape-shifting trickster with the voice of the schmuck in the cubicle next door. He might be our savior. He might be the guy in the black robe holding the scythe. He might be both. . . . Each poem is a little narrative. Sometimes the story is a commonplace, even tedious account, and sometimes it shocks with the absolute strangeness of its familiarity. In each case the same nonjudgmental voice delivers the news—the bad news—that if we're not careful, we will go mad inside our hypernormal lives."

David Baker, poetry editor of the *Kenyon Review* and author of *Never-Ending Bird*, from his foreword

Staring at the Cracks in the Wall

I think I've stared at people and objects for most of my life. It's my nature, I guess, to be standing around at a party and staring at cracks in the walls or the lines in people's faces when they tell a story, or noting the sounds and the physical movements they make when they talk.

In November of 1987, I started writing in a composition book. I didn't know what I was doing. I felt compelled to write something because a friend of mine wrote in his composition book. I wrote poetry extensively in college and over the next two decades, but none of it felt right. The poems weren't going anywhere. As soon as I had them on paper, they were dead. I made statements about objects and people, and I stated my feelings, or some sort of rot. I have those poems around here, but I never look at them.

In 2007, after ten years of writing tight newspaper stories on extreme deadline and noting everything I've ever feared or was nervous about, I started writing different poems. I used moments during my day job, lunchtime in the truck, or late at night when everyone was asleep. This work was different. I think I had finally gotten my formula right: Everything I've ever stared at, meditated on, watched, or studied was worked into what I was writing. Anything went. I stayed out of the way.

Most of the poetry I write is based on what I've seen—something I stared at yesterday is placed next to something I saw when I was a kid. These images might be layered with whatever angst, fear, dread, or rage that I'm experiencing at any moment. Through this process, the poems seem alive enough and free enough to fly all over the place.

Worthy Evans

A Funny Thing †

My secret fell out from the cuff of my pants
just as I walked up to take the award
for best-dressed, most improved, fullest
all-around role model for the underprivileged,
old people and kids. Everyone stared at my secret,
a pile near the podium set for me to speak.
The clapping died down. There I stood,
all khaki slacks and casual pullover,
looking into thousands of eyes.
I sidled up to the podium, adjusted
the microphone. I wasn't what they said
I was. I never played football. I last made
an honor roll in eighth grade. I learned history
from *Mad* magazines, opera
from Looney Toons, literature from
the Beaver's dad. I can't even find
the degree the college gave me. Busting my knee
in the army kept me out of Korea
and put me on a long road home, where
the SUVs aren't V-8s, aren't even all-wheel drive.
The plantations are neighborhoods.
The bricks amount to a façade. I put everything
on credit and haven't the cash to back it up.
I went on for hours. I must've offended
someone, but no one sitting in the amphitheater
left. I drank all the water the podium

people left for me and was still thirsty.
The crowd walked out, looking intent, as
if they had people of all ages to save. I picked up
my secret from the stage and put it in my back
pocket. Everyone knew what it was now.

Comfort †

Every summer afternoon I get
a whiff of my own scent. I
smell like sweaty woolen socks,

day-old underwear, wet
cotton and muffled farts.
Other people swear they

can't smell whatever it is
that I'm smelling on me,
but that's OK. I know they

are lying. They are being good
neighbors and are keeping a secret.
Everyone knows they love me,

but let's keep calm. Work must get done.

Making the Man

Other people wear clothes that
I like, but I try them on and they
never fit. The clothes that fit
make me look like a father, even
if I'm walking into a hotel three
hundred miles from home.
Other people fell out of the hotel
through the years, either because
they wanted to or someone pushed.
I go outside to a sandwich shop
a block away to get the fallen people
out of my head, but after the sandwich
I still have to walk back to the
hotel. I still have to go home wearing
the clothes I have. My shirts balloon.
Shorts too tight in the waist, too loose
in the crotch. Shoes are comfortable,
but trip over wires and kick
against walls. People live better
inside clothes I give up regularly, hoping
I fit somewhere in a home, the way
people fit inside their homes.

Heroes in Waiting

I felt a sickness in the back of my
throat when I woke up. I popped
a pill and went into the shower. By
the time I got to work the sickness
reached my stomach, but I had
no couch on which to fall. We
had to see about changes in
a computer application that
weren't in the program yesterday.
None of us knew exactly what to
do. The poster said we were
heroes in waiting and needed a pat
on the back. Teamwork classes
included catching each other as we're
falling off of porches. All of us, though,
gathered around a big box and put
our hands in. What we felt, we
had to fix. But first we had to
identify what it was we held.
I became dizzy, delirious, fumbling
around over necks or nuggets
of unknown substance. Hero worship
put on hold. I fell to the floor with
all of these arms touching me,
finding me out.

Baked into the Cake

The bride was kissed. The cake
was eaten. Lula had completed
her customary belly dance and
there arose such an emotional
reception that tears came to my
eyes in delight. As these things do,
the good feeling died down and I
caught on to the one-way conversation
about doorknobs. Phillip the
bartender, he listened in too, after
serving me up a gin and tonic.
Marshall Weinstein, of the Kensington
Weinsteins, had clinked a glass and
begun the downhill slide into doorknobs.
*Sometimes we encounter crystal
doorknobs that you need only push
to open the door, which had long since
swelled beyond the jamb.* I began
to feel ill. *Brass ones gleam brightly,
but oh, the polishing that we must
do.* Marshall was up front, beside
Regina Whittingham, nee Winkleman,
and I was near the door at this
reception in the basement of a redone
barn. There were no doorknobs here.

The iron doorknobs with patterns
stamped upon them turn black over
time, get lost in sock drawers, where
little children mistake them for turtles.
He laughed at this, maybe remembering
some unprompted discovery after his dad
had gone to work. I remember missing
Lula's belly dancing, so in a twist in my chair,
I looked out the unlatched door at a mother
hen waddling around with her chicks.
My son isn't going to like her.

Green Revolver

Four weeks ago Matthew moved
some bones from the back yard
to the front yard. Three weeks ago he
helped his mom around the house,
picking up laundry, throwing loose paper
away. She gave him two dollars.
Two weeks ago I took him
to a dollar store. Matthew walked back
to the wall of dime toys and found
a green revolver, little gray blackjack
and gold handcuffs, shrink-wrapped against
an upbeat cardboard law-enforcement sign.
One week ago he climbed into the truck
with his revolver that he constantly
clicked. He left it there when I pushed him
out for school, and it sits here right now,
on the seat. Every person talking about work
on the walking trail, every mocking bird,
every passing car, click, click, click.

The Madman's Divining Time

After the rain, we walked out onto
the patio. The air was still wet
and the bark of the fat pine tree
was streaked with hits and misses. I've never
seen our backyard so green and liquid.
Mona checked her plants to see
if the passing shower gave them anything
at all. She worked her thumbs into the pots
of petunias, pansies, marigolds
whatever they were, a wild palate of color
mixed and matched by a madman.
He has a plan for us, Mona said.
With each shower he carves us up
into little pieces and shows us colors we
never knew we were. I looked down
at the thin puddle on the porch. In the twilight
I was a muddle of ruddy bumps
and sandy dribbles of gray hair.
Mona, of course, showed herself in blues and
oranges, ochre, velvety red, peach,
jasmine and touches of deep purple
where the setting sun steals the other colors
away. Maybe, if I worked the dirt up
under my fingernails, there
would be hope for me. Mona had
already left the deck and soared off into the
leftover sunshine to dance with that fiend.

PART 6

Excavation (2011)

Jennifer Pournelle

"The excavations that take place in this book are literal and metaphorical. As the speaker moves through Europe, the Middle East, and the American Southwest, she's undertaking a serious study of the brick and mortar composition of cities such as Vienna, Berlin, San Diego, and Baghdad. But each city is, as the speaker notes, 'a city within a city,' that is, a story within a story, the layers of which come to light as the speaker soaks up each environment—its textures, its temperatures, its temperaments—its past offenses, its present troubles, and its future possibilities."

Rigoberto Gonzalez, author of *Butterfly Boy: Memories of a Chicano Mariposa*, from his foreword

Urban Excavations

These poems are excerpted from *Excavation: A City Cycle*——an extended reflection on how cities layer and blend past, present, and future throughout their construction and among their citizens.

Coscoy, Renamed San Diego is a love poem to my hometown. It, like me, was and is shaped by the great ocean waves that bore and commingled immigrant waves from time immemorial with immigrant waves from Spain and Italy, and through them (and subsequent to them) from the Middle East, North Africa, and a hundred other shores. To San Diego, great ships of exploration came across world oceans; from San Diego, great ships of war depart to patrol those selfsame seas. It is the city from which I have set out on great adventures, and to which I have always returned. It could be any port city, really: it reminds me most of Charleston, at the same latitude, on America's opposite shore.

Jerusalem was selected from the section "Babylon"——a fractured tour of multiple cities in the Middle East. It summarizes my reflections on the disintegration of the great promise of unification held out to Europe at the end of the Cold War. It was written while working on several projects aimed at bringing stability and hope to the part of the world that has inspired great writing and great religions since urban life began. As at the Tower of Babel, great achievement was undone by miscommunication, greed, and conflicting vision.

Baghdad, When a Church Is Bombed was written while I worked on reconstruction projects in Iraq in 2003–4. The city still struggles to come to grips with its new present and old pasts. It is, in a very real sense, the successor city of the once-great Babylon. We hope that, like Vienna or Berlin—two other cities "excavated" in the book—some new great city will arise from the rubble of war.

Jennifer Pournelle

Coscoy, Renamed San Diego de Alcala, 1602 *

San Diego, 1993—96

I

There's a city within the city
Where Kumeyaay sifted tidal silt for clambakes;
pounded river bark to ribbons dyed with purple shells and
    desert ochres;
marked their lips with colors strained from cactus flowers
and traded heavy baskets loaded high with salt-dried fish
for Chumash drugs and palm hearts; prickly pear and
    acorn flour;
for gourds aslosh with sour mescal, the pounding, kneading,
    rolling, scraping
of stone on stone and palms on bread
in tempo with the washing tides to mark the days and hours;
Baskets woven,
bark skirts beaded,
hair roped and larded,
caves and cliffs and rocky faces
painted with the wheels of heaven;
with cycles, suns, and stars——

II

There's a city within the city
even within this city,
laid stucco wall to stucco wall
on grizzled earth scraped clean as seabeds
newly planed to lifelessness by shrimpers' nets.
Where Cabrillo stood on Coscoy's mounds
above reed-choked marshes soon to be malarial
and Fra Serra planted first his Spanish cross——
here, where traffic flows like water never roared,
the slow and brackish estuary
chuffing green beneath the freeway trusses
like light from far-flung stars arriving now so brilliantly,
so long and far away from where the stars themselves
    blinked out——

III

There's a city within the city,
where missions, tiled and stuccoed, rose;
immense adobe barracks, square as Karak citadel,
built in triumph once the Moors seized Palestine,
flash-flooding west as conquerors on stone-paved Roman roads,
a relentless dust storm lashing hard,
blown across North Africa,
their plows replacing Spanish plows;
their colored tiles and Arabesques
and plaster, brilliant white on softening domes,
encrusting Roman villa courts;
their horses, foreheads marked with stars,
plunging past the pagan horns of fighting bulls
beneath the flashing pants of Catholic picadors——

IV

There's a city within the city
here, where soldiers, priests, and farmers
with no need of cities, acorn groves, or clam nets
first plowed-under coastal scrub for buildings,
then plowed down their makeshift walls and kicked aside
    shell middens
for the fortress carried brick by brick within their heads along
    Crusader marches,
struggling against the Indians
compressing at the speed of light a thousand years of city
    growth
to half a century here.

Here, where rivers slog their brackish way
to vast, undrinkable lapping seas;
        to Dead Seas,
        Red Seas,
blue as mosque tiles against the chaparral dust,
here, forests—
submerged and wavering browns of kelp beds tiled with
    abalone,
no use in crafting ship masts or hulls——
here, finally
halting Moors and Crusaders both—

V

There's a city within this city,
in this hostile place so welcome; known;
salt and scent enticing officers; reformers; revolutionary guards
to build a home away from home
then plot in darkened houses to upset the status quo
and break the chain that stretched across vast oceans
from their legionary outpost here to Jordan's citadels;
their campaigns beset by fevers
loaded with the cattle, wheat, and corn, and goats
amassed in holds with Canton silk and Plymouth tea
all dumped at dockside, then dispersed
to stud the land with life regrown
in farmer's plots and stick-plowed fields
atop the strip-mined desert soil—

VI

There's a city within this city,
here, the citadels abandoned
for the market gardens, shipping docks, and garrisons
all set alongside royal bells
to mark new causeways north and south—
letters, baggage, governments,
all flashing past on stage stops,
the clattering of the teamsters' hooves
echoing through the warehouses;
the marshes drained to riverbeds,
the rivers dammed and waters sucked
to olive roots, alfalfa fields;
to vineyards, herds, and greenhouses;
sent gushing over citrus groves.
Flowering almonds from Jordan's hills on these hills now,
their petals witness to railroad spurs,
then rails,
then stations;
then concrete spires and stucco towers,
raised above the charnel strips
left by brush fires whipping mules and horses,
         burros, ghettos,
         fields and ghost towns
         grasslands, homes
spilling onto back lots,
engulfing movie sets;
replayed in news clips every summer's end—

VII

There's a city within this city,
this city once raised up,
then pulled back down again,
the flash of starlight winking out,
but excavated still from trash heaps:
      bath tiles,
      broken shards of Fiesta plates
resurrected bright in stucco spires
of rebar filigreed with arabesques and Byzantine mosaic—

Through all of this, the waters flowed;
the adz and plow and bulldoze blade
following on the slower wax of sunlight
glinting past from miners pans and fishers' baskets
out into the Moorish court of seas,
arriving only now on Roman shores;
the sighs of waves not sighs at all,
but washing hands rocked back and forth;
but woven baskets stirred and swayed
to separate the day from weed—

VIII

There's a city within the city.
It beats alive in shrimpers' hearts
with hearty mounds of seabed scraped
from light-years past and roasted, steamed, piled into mouths
at seafood feasts in stucco style,
served up by children hence long mixed
of conquering and conquered——
still tending squash-sprawled gardens
far below the midden mounds;
still trading foodstuffs east and south,
and strolling hand to hand through shopping malls
the cactus colors of their lips; the desert ochres of their caves
kiln-fired across the Spanish tiles
encrusted over Anglo courts erected here in angles; towers;
in mezzanines and breezeways lined
with shop doors hawking Canton silks,
and English teas in linen bags, and holograms, and plastic
    purple carryalls——

It bolts across the freeway lanes
traversing estuary reeds,
comes north on causeways loaded down
with woven cloth, not beaten flat from river bark
but spun from fibers traded here from ship holds;
dyed in wild pastels stuccoed high on deco walls,
the kiss of native cactus lips
the art of Chumash shaman hands
the seed and sex and wealth and eyes still coming here from
distant lands so long since lost to time——

IX

There's a city within the city.
It's sanitized in Old Town;
bastardized and vilified on Avenida Revolucion;
it whirls in bright Casino lights, new stars winked on above
the wheels of chance that spin and tempt
in gaming halls and Indian saloons;
it stares at us from muleteer eyes
caught burning black in daguerreotype;
we catch its smell in lard-soaked stands
that sell fish tacos, freshly spritzed with lime.

The city here that burns within beckons fresh from gallery
    doors;
it lies exposed in fossil seams that mark the ancient midden
    mounds;
it glimmers in the neon signs and hangs in braids on blond
    girls' backs;
it crashes in the concert halls
and dances on the table tops to Mariachi bands——

X

There's a city within the city.
And where the city lives, we live,
and eat and sing and drink and laugh,
and love, and war, and cry;
we tender oceanic nets, imagining like kelp beds that
we feel the movement of the spheres,
so now, built up from all that was,
we are,
like commentary tales that come
from planetary depths long gone.

Jerusalem ✳

Jerusalem, 1993

The crack of a rifle
The crack of a bone

As if hammering a small boy's arm
with the very rock he threw——
his face twisted in a cowl of tears;
the hammerer, at twice his size,
a mask of earnest endeavor—

As if hammering, the thudding dull
        before the crack along the arm
were work: enduring, new, profound:
a way of mending torn up stones
a way of mending pounded arms
a way of mending lungs torn hot
from busloads by fanatic arms:
wired to detonators, pinned to ribs,
their last, wet break a bloody implosion;
        a crack,
        a spring,
        and then a roar,
and then no sound.

PART 7

Hold Like Owls (2012)

Julia Koets

"Koets has a penchant for surprising metaphor. She possesses a personal delight for the highest flying verbs and their alluring descriptors. . . . I am grateful to this poet for this first book of poems. I am grateful for what she has taken the time to remind me of. She is just getting started. I applaud the alphabet spilling from her hands."

> Nikky Finney, winner of the National Book award
> and author of *Head Off & Split*, from her foreword

Stitching the Sides of a Story Together

Some poems take years to write, to realize the significance of various memories and images; others come quickly. I wrote a complete first draft of "Shrug of Broken Egg, Frozen Shell" late one night at my friends' kitchen table, while they made ice cubes. On the other hand, "Joy, the Elephant, Greenville Zoo, 1990" draws from my childhood memories of the dust and heat and wonder of going to the zoo with my grandmother and my younger brother.

Poetry can try to make sense of the folds in a woman's dress and tell you without hesitation that all you need to know of a man are the lines that make him. In a poem the sky can be tired, a church can be broken-down, and a highway field can turn as red as a girl's hair.

Many of these poems selected for this anthology from my book, *Hold Like Owls*, contain images that are embedded in my memories of growing up in the South, sitting on the back steps, driving past old houses hollowed out, living where the lake and trees are big enough. For me, poetry, both reading and writing it, is about stitching the sides of a story together.

Whether writing about personal histories, language, or longing, I find myself writing poems that allow for questioning and uncertainty to exist.

Julia Koets

Woman Drawn with Stars

Mucha painted a woman with red flowers
about her head to match her lips and the beads

down her neck. To rest your cheek against
your palm is to wonder where planes go

when extinct. They rust in the sky. They let
their parts fall back to Earth. There are so many
stars I cannot connect. Sink deeper, painted

woman, into this chair of cloth and wine
until the pattern of folds
down your robe makes sense.

Bruise ✴

I often drove over a hill with a girl
        where our town turned
into another, past scattered tractor parts,
        house hollowed out, a wandering dog,
a chiropractor sign made from real back bones.

Parked by a strip mall, her voice fit inside
        a chestnut shell. She told me she never wanted
to talk in a parking lot.
        She would sit in a house where walls
could hear us
        figuring it out in the small
of the South's back. We were too afraid
to kiss a woman, then,
until it bruised, wore us
down to girls
we no longer recognized.

Beauty Secrets ✳

In plastic lawn chairs next to the lake
we pour olive oil in our hands and run our fingers
through our hair: a beauty secret you'd read quickly
in a grocery line magazine. We take turns wrapping

each other's hair in flowered scarves, tied
at the back. At ten you knew how vitamin E could
cover a face: habit you'd watched your mother
keep before she went to bed. And you joke,

at thirty, that that's why your dad left your mom
when you were twenty and gone to L.A. for sun
and school. It's ok,   I don't know how to say.
But you already know: the lake and trees are big
enough here to keep the secrets that won't leave.

Oconee Bells

Its lace requires fine thread,
and white petals that can be pressed
to paper stars between heavy pages
of my parents' *Collier's Encyclopedia*.

Ten years ago two men flew
around the world in a silver balloon,
and the gray whale
was no longer endangered.
Whoever finds this book
in the piles upstairs
might search the name

of these flowers that a book says
were once lost for a hundred years;
and their searching will stitch
the sides of these bells, again.

Hold like Owls

You wear your hair like curtains, drawn down
to sigh, a word you could go on without
translating, breath the throat can't own

and chest won't keep. Your eyes hold like owls,
but they're blue: the difference
between the bird and girl. Rocks drawn down

a mountain leave shadows of your face, found
centuries before. It's too dark to tell if pink
held your cheeks even then. Throat can't own

what's in the air. The sky's as tired as you are now
and have been before. Why do you think the river
holds so many stones? Wear your hair down

your shoulder. The air singing clings to, mouths
won't bottle for tiny ships. No, the birds still
wander without translating arias of their own.

Wings look effortless. Try singing out loud
and mouth the words that won't come, until
you wear your hair like curtains, drawn down
to curl against your cheeks, a score of its own.

My Quixote

All that you need to know of a man are the lines
that make him: the sun is a circle; the sword
is a straight line; the horizon, broken; the wind,
in between. I watch him twist the thin string

of a teabag around his finger with the rugged
gentleness of horses or a beard. He rests
his cup on his wearing jeans and tells me the trees
that line the highway fields turned red as a girl's

hair: impractical as all things that fall. I wrap
both hands around my warm mug until they meet
and move closer to him on the back steps.

Joy, the Elephant,
Greenville Zoo, 1990

Her cage was the one at the top of the hill: pool
dirty with upcountry clay, two tires scattered
in dust, a few blocks of hay to keep the ground
from running when it rained. Thick-skinned

and dry, beast which Aristotle wrote
passeth all others in wit and mind, accompanied
the lonely river my grandmother walked
with my brother and me some Saturdays.

She danced by herself in the rise and fall
of a one-two-three, the drag of her feet, her heavy
trunk and tusks in the afternoon. In the mail years
later, my grandmother wrote that Joy had died:

a newspaper photograph showed her gait,
her widening eyes. She looked quite weightless,
as I remember, a sort of waltz in her thighs.

December Hemlock

The trees are safe in the cold, white sort
      of grieving covering a field; ground only
flawed at the edge of the road
      where cars turn white to mud.

She counts the hemlock rings at the trunk
      where beavers cut back
through years. The ponds have turned
      to spilled milk, but no one would hear
her crying out here in the woods, quiet with snow.

Ruin

for Amy

Praise the wind heavy with frying onion and dust
      that covers us in the streets of Athens. I had thought

I was a fool to think this place could save us.
      Place apart, where art is old. But the two of us sitting

on this cold marble floor in a broken-down
      church find something in the faded Byzantine

scenes on its walls. Hands and breath have changed
      the paint, reds gone to orange with age and praise.

CONTRIBUTORS

DéLana R. A. Dameron won the 2008 South Carolina Poetry Book Prize, selected by Elizabeth Alexander for *How God Ends Us*. Dameron's poetry has appeared in numerous journals and anthologies, including *African American Review, ESSENCE Magazine, The Ringing Ear: Black Poets Lean South, PMS: PoemMemoirStory, 42opus, storySouth, Pembroke Magazine,* and *Borderlands: Texas Poetry Review*. She has received fellowships from New York University, the Cave Canem Foundation, Soul Mountain, and the Constance Saltonstall Foundation for the Arts. A native of Columbia, South Carolina, Dameron currently resides in New York City.

Kwame Dawes is a professor of English at the University of Nebraska and the Glenna Luschei Editor of the *Prairie Schooner*. A prolific author, he has published more than thirty works, including poetry collections, short stories, nonfiction, novels, drama, and critical articles. He has been honored with numerous awards, such as the Barnes and Nobles Poets and Writers for Writers Award, a Guggenheim Fellowship for Literature, and an Emmy Award for New Approaches to News and Documentary. His most recent works include *Wheels, Home Is Where: An Anthology of African American Poetry from the Carolinas,* and *Back of Mount Peace*.

The 2009 winner of the South Carolina Poetry Prize for his collection, *Green Revolver* (selected by David Baker), **Worthy Evans** is a 1994 graduate of the College of Charleston with a bachelor's degree in history. He enlisted in the army after graduation and was stationed at Fort Hood, Texas. He drove armored personnel carriers, blew up things, and kept records for his unit's vehicles. In his off time he drove all over Texas and did not write much. After the army, Evans served as a sports writer for four newspapers, the *Winnsboro Herald-Independent,* the *Beaufort Gazette,* the *State,* and the *Sumter Item*. He is currently a communications specialist for a

101

Medicare contractor in Columbia, where he balances writing poetry, collage making, and anything else that comes along with work. Evans is married with two children.

Julia Koets holds an MFA from the University of South Carolina, Columbia. Her poetry has appeared in numerous journals, including *Indiana Review, Los Angeles Review, Euphony,* and *Cutthroat: A Journal of the Arts.* Koets, a native of Summerville, South Carolina, currently resides in San Francisco, California. Her poetry collection, *Hold for Owls,* was the winner of the 2010 South Carolina Poetry Book Prize (selected by Nikky Finney) and was published by the University of South Carolina Press in 2012.

An associate professor of English at the University of South Carolina and a writer in residence at the Riverbanks Botanical Gardens in Columbia, **Ed Madden** is the author of three books of poetry. His first collection, *Signals,* won the 2007 South Carolina Poetry Book Prize. A second collection, *Prodigal: Variations,* was published in 2011, and a third, *Nest,* is forthcoming from Salmon in Ireland. His poems have appeared in *Arkansas Review, Los Angeles Review, Poetry Ireland,* and other journals, as well as in *Best New Poets 2007* and the Notre Dame anthology *The Book of Irish American Poetry from the Eighteenth Century to the Present.* He is also the author of *Tiresian Poetics: Modernism, Sexuality, Voice 1888–2001,* a study of sexuality and modernist literature, and co-editor with Marti Lee of *Irish Studies: Geographies and Genders.* In 2010 he was the winner of the South Carolina Academy of Authors inaugural Carrie McCray Nickens fellowship.

Ray McManus is the author of three books of poetry: *Driving through the Country before You Are Born* (winner of the South Carolina First Book Prize, University of South Carolina Press, 2007 selected by Kate Daniels), *Left Behind* (a winner of the South Carolina Poetry Initiative chapbook prize, 2008), and *Red Dirt Jesus* (winner of the Marick Press Poetry Prize, 2011). His poetry has appeared in many journals such as *Nimrod, Los Angeles Review, Crazyhorse, Asheville Poetry Review, Borderlands,* and *Arkansas Review,* and he has performed his poetry nationally and internationally. When he is not reading or performing his work around the country, Ray teaches creative writing, Irish literature, rhetoric, and composition as an assistant professor of English in the Division of Arts and Letters at University of South Carolina, Sumter.

Susan Laughter Meyers is the author of *Keep and Give Away*, selected by Terrance Hayes for the inaugural South Carolina Poetry Book Prize. It also won the Southern Independent Booksellers Alliance (SIBA) Book Award for Poetry and the Brockman-Campbell Book Award. Her chapbook, *Lessons in Leaving*, was selected by Brendan Galvin for the 1998 Persephone Press Book Award. Her poetry has also been published by numerous journals, including the *Southern Review, Beloit Poetry Journal,* and *Prairie Schooner,* as well as *Poetry Daily, Verse Daily,* and Ted Kooser's "American Life in Poetry." Honors include fellowships from the South Carolina Academy of Authors and the Virginia Center for the Creative Arts. A long-time writing instructor with an MFA from Queens University of Charlotte, Meyers currently teaches workshops and classes in community programs. She has served as president of the poetry societies of both North and South Carolina and as chair of the North Carolina Writers Conference. She lives with her husband in the rural community of Givhans, South Carolina.

Jennifer R. Pournelle has lived in ten states and eight countries. She received her doctorate in anthropology and archaeology from the University of California, San Diego. After leaving the U.S. Army, she spent time as a professional editor before embarking on her current career as an environmental anthropologist and archaeologist. Her work in Turkey, Iraq, and the Caucasus has been featured in the *New York Times* and on the *Discovery Channel* and *National Geographic Television*. Her poems have appeared in *Parnassus Literary Journal* and *Minerva*. She lives with her partner in Columbia, South Carolina, where Pournelle is a research assistant professor with the University of South Carolina Environment and Sustainability Program. Pournelle is the author of *Outies,* a new work of science fiction, and was the 2010 recipient of the South Carolina Poetry Initiative Book Prize for *Excavations: A City Cycle,* which was selected by Rigoberto Gonzalez.

Marjory Wentworth's poems have been nominated for the Push-cart Prize five times. Her books of poetry include *Noticing Eden, Despite Gravity, The Endless Repetition of an Ordinary Miracle,* and *What the Water Gives Me.* Her award-winning book *Shackles,* is a children's story. *Taking a Stand: The Evolution of Human Rights* by Juan Méndez with Marjory Wentworth was published in September 2011. She is the Poet Laureate of South Carolina, and she teaches at the Art Institute of Charleston and Roper St. Francis Hospital.

portraits
spiritual
death
relationship
allegory
abstracts → feelings & images
litural & metaphorical

CPSIA information can be obtained at www.ICGtesting.com
Printed in the USA
LVOW040508061112

306028LV00002B/1/P